Meet the
Masters

An INTERVIEW

with **PLATO**

Donald R. Moor

Cavendish
Square

New York

Published in 2015 by Cavendish Square Publishing, LLC
243 5th Avenue, Suite 136, New York, NY 10016

First Edition

Website: cavendishsq.com

This publication represents the opinions and views of the author based on his or her personal experience, knowledge, and research. The information in this book serves as a general guide only. The author and publisher have used their best efforts in preparing this book and disclaim liability rising directly or indirectly from the use and application of this book.

CPSIA Compliance Information: Batch #WS14CSQ

All websites were available and accurate when this book was sent to press.

Library of Congress Cataloging-in-Publication Data

Moor, Donald R.
An interview with Plato / by Donald R. Moor.
p. cm. — (Meet the masters)
Includes index.
ISBN 978-1-62712-906-0 (hardcover) ISBN 978-1-62712-908-4 (ebook)
1. Plato — Juvenile literature. 2. Philosophers — Greece — Biography — Juvenile literature. 3. Greece — History — To 146 B.C. — Juvenile literature. I. Title.
B393.M66 2015
184—d23

Editorial Director: Dean Miller
Senior Editor: Fletcher Doyle
Senior Copy Editor: Wendy A. Reynolds
Art Director: Jeffrey Talbot

Designer: Amy Greenan
Production Manager: Jennifer Ryder-Talbot
Production Editor: David McNamara
Photo Research: J8 Media

Printed in the United States of America

CONTENTS

FOREWORD

by Robert M. Pirsig

There is an old **Hindu** story about a fish that searches high and low, and far and wide, to find this mysterious thing he has heard of called "water," but he searches and searches and never finds it. The same problem occurs when we try to find Plato. It is so hard to find where Plato is because it is so hard to find where Plato is not. We live inside the mind of Plato. Whenever we reason about things dialectically, we are imitating Plato. As Alfred North Whitehead has said, "The safest generalization that can be made about the history of Western **philosophy** is that it is all a series of footnotes to Plato."

When attorneys argue a case before a court, they are reenacting Plato's **dialectic**. When the board of directors of a corporation decides which direction to take the company, it also is reenacting the **dialogues** of Plato. When a parliament or congress convenes to decide the future of a nation, it adheres to Plato's rules. Even when we "debate" privately in our own minds what we want to do next with our lives, that "debate" is a dialogue of Plato.

When we go to school we are actually entering a descendant of Plato's original **Academy**, and what we learn there is what Socrates and Plato taught: Always keep an open mind. Consider many answers, and carefully examine each answer to see which seems best. Do not use emotion

Statues of Socrates (left) and Plato loom over the site of the Academy in Athens, Greece. Socrates was Plato's inspiration for starting the Academy.

to arrive at this answer. Do not threaten force to make others agree with you. Reason thoughtfully and calmly and choose from these answers which one seems the best way to conduct your life, and if you do this not only your own life but the lives of others around will become better and better.

What Socrates, Plato, and their followers (as well as some of the pre-Socratic philosophers) were establishing was a whole new intellectual level of belief: that knowledge, logic, and the art of argument were sufficient to guide the world. Today, all this seems so natural and obvious that it is hard to see that someone had to sit down and actually invent it. But look at what the world was like before Plato was born, look at other countries today where Plato's way of reasoning has never been understood, and you will see what an enormous gift this philosopher has left to all of us.

When we study Plato, what we are most likely to see are his differences from our modern way of thinking, and it is normal to think that he is wrong and we are right. However, one can benefit greatly by following his advice to keep an open mind. Try to see what forces caused him to reason the way he did. And perhaps speculate on what people will think of our own beliefs and customs 2,400 years from now.

INTRODUCTION

The central place that Plato occupies in the European philosophical tradition is due to a number of factors. He was the first Western philosopher whose works have survived intact. These works have remained influential because of their wide scope, their incisive reasoning, and their power to engage readers. Plato's frequent use of literary devices—myths, metaphors, and **allegories**—has succeeded in enticing readers who might have been less attentive to bare **treatises**.

Plato did not speak in his own voice, but had the characters of his dialogues speak for themselves—in this way presenting readers with a variety of philosophical perspectives. By holding himself in the background he left room for radically different interpretations of his works, from the otherworldly religious doctrines of the **Neoplatonists** to the severely anti-metaphysical notions of present-day analytic philosophers.

In this imagined conversation, however, Plato is invited to speak for himself. These dialogues avoid almost entirely the literary devices that have given rise to the religious and metaphysical ideas that are so often associated with him. Nearly all of the discussion is focused on the fundamental social, political, and philosophical issues on which it is quite certain that Plato held definite views. Here, we meet Plato on the ground that matters to us all.

1

PLATO: HIS LIFE IN SHORT

By 427 BCE, Athens had achieved the glory for which it is known and begun the struggle that led to its decline. Most of the great monumental architecture had been completed: the **Parthenon** graced the **Acropolis**, and the temple of Hephaestus dominated the metalworkers' district. The leading dramatists' works were performed in the theaters. Aeschylus had been dead for a generation, Sophocles was at the height of his career, and Euripides had produced his first plays.

A substantial empire had been assembled. The Delian league, a defensive maritime alliance, had been transformed into an association dominated by Athens. The city was becoming the intellectual center of the Greek world. **Sophists**—itinerant teachers of **rhetoric**—were challenging established ways of thinking. Among them, Protagoras was the most provocative, teaching that there is no distinction between appearance and reality, and expressing doubts as to whether the gods existed. Native Athenians, including the barefoot philosopher Socrates, contributed to the intellectual ferment.

Casting what may have been a still imperceptible shadow over the city was the Peloponnesian war against the **Spartan** alliance. By 427 BCE, the war was just four years old, but it had already cost Athens dearly. Its citizens

A view from the south of the Parthenon, one of the architectural masterpieces of ancient Greece.

under siege, the city had been struck by a plague that had reduced the population by a quarter and had taken its great democratic leader, Pericles. These misfortunes were only the start of the sufferings the long war visited upon the Athenians.

Not the least of the costs of the war was an intensification of the rivalry between the supporters of the democracy that Pericles had led and the **aristocracy**. Among the leading families of the aristocracy was the one into which, around 428 or 427 BCE, Plato was born. His given name was Aristocles, though he was known from his youth by the nickname under which he would become famous. His siblings were two older brothers, Glaucon and Adeimantus, and a sister, Potone. While he was very young his father died, and his mother married her uncle. Unlike his other relatives, Plato's stepfather had connections with the democratic party, having been an associate of Pericles.

As a member of the aristocracy, Plato enjoyed the privilege of wealth—and no doubt had the benefit of the best education. He was almost certainly schooled in mathematics, music, and poetry. His written works are sprinkled with quotations from Homer and other poets. Diogenes Laërtius, who lived several centuries after Plato but had access to earlier records, tells of Plato having written a play that he meant to enter in a competition. This play he is said to have destroyed after he had become familiar with the ideas of Socrates (469–399 BCE). The example of Socrates, a humble ex-stonecutter demolishing the pretensions to wisdom of the "wise men" of Greece made an enormous impression on the teenaged Plato. Socrates' quests for satisfactory definitions of justice, courage, wisdom, and the like led Plato eventually to see these as the essence of philosophy. The body of thought

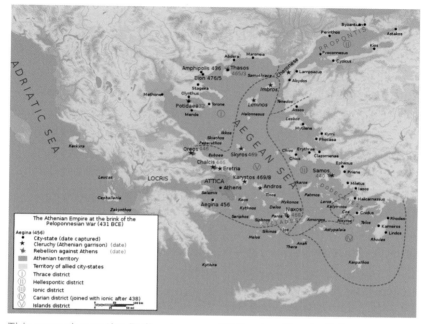

This map shows the Delian League ("Athenian Empire") in 431 BCE, just prior to the Peloponnesian War.

that we know as **Platonism** is based on the distinction between these abstract natures and the concrete individuals who possess them.

The war with the Spartan alliance continued off and on throughout Plato's childhood and youth, until it ended in the defeat of Athens in 404 BCE. There is little reliable information about Plato's youth, but it is reported that he was an accomplished wrestler, and it is very likely that he rendered military service during the late years of the war. Because of his status, he would probably have served in the cavalry.

After the Athenian surrender in 404 BCE, the Spartans imposed upon Athens the rulership of a group of thirty men from the Athenian aristocracy. Among the leaders of the faction were two of Plato's relatives, his second cousin Critias, and Charmides, his uncle. Young Plato was invited to join this governing body, but he hesitated, wanting first to see how they ruled. Within months it was clear that they were earning the name by which history has known them, "The Thirty Tyrants." The lawlessness with which they conducted themselves horrified Plato. Their wholesale killings and banishments, and the attempts to implicate every prominent citizen in their crimes, repelled Plato so much that he welcomed the victory of the democrats in the civil war that broke out in 403 BCE. Both Critias and Charmides were killed during these hostilities. Critias's death left the Thirty without a leader, and the **junta** collapsed. Nothing is recorded of Plato's feelings about the deaths in battle of his kinsmen, both of whom he later pictured favorably in his dialogues.

Although the leaders of the democracy were magnanimous in their treatment of their vanquished rivals, they soon lost the allegiance of the 28-year-old Plato when, in 399 BCE, they put Socrates to death on charges of impiety and corrupting the young. Disillusioned with his own city, Plato is reported to have then spent about a dozen years traveling. He first visited the nearby city of Megara, where he found congenial company among former companions of Socrates. He later visited the mathematician Eudoxus in Cyrene, North Africa, and in southern Italy the Pythagorean community, some members of which he had known as companions of Socrates in Athens.

For no reason that has been recorded, he traveled to Syracuse in Sicily. There he met a young man who was to become one of his dearest friends and greatest admirers: Dion, the brother-in-law of the tyrant Dionysius I. He was

Plato's Academy, depicted in this painting by Raphael, attracted the finest minds in the Greek world.

intellectually able and much interested in Plato's philosophy, especially his thoughts on government.

After this long absence Plato returned to Athens, and in 387 BCE he founded the Academy on the outskirts of the city. He gathered there an array of the finest minds in the Greek world. The geometer Eudoxus was one of the most prominent of the early members, but younger mathematicians also achieved renown for their work there. Plato named one of his dialogues after Theaetetus, who had achieved a wide reputation when he was killed in battle at a relatively young age. Another "home-grown" mathematician was Plato's own nephew, Speusippus. Of course, the most famous member of the Academy was the philosopher Aristotle, who arrived from Macedonia, where his father was physician to the king. Aristotle came at the age of eighteen as a student, and remained until Plato's death twenty years later.

No substantial records remain of the activities that took place at the Academy, but it is certain that both mathematics and philosophy were pursued vigorously and at the highest level. Questions of natural science, including astronomy, seem also to have occupied the academicians. The extraordinary range of Aristotle's interests may well reflect the breadth of the topics addressed there.

Both during Plato's lifetime and for centuries after, the Academy played a large role in the advancement of mathematics. Solid geometry was advanced by Theaetetus, who established that there are only five solids whose faces are all identical regular polygons—called the five Platonic solids. Plato's insistence that mathematics should be built on firmly established foundations is likely to have led eventually to Euclid's systematization of geometry a century later.

Plato apparently delivered lectures on philosophical topics. Aristotle tells of the occasion on which Plato lectured on the good. The topic attracted a large audience—most of whom, according to Aristotle, were greatly disappointed when they were subjected to a lengthy discourse filled with mathematics. Aristotle was almost alone at the end of the lecture. It is hard to know what to make of this report, since Plato was obviously a successful leader of the Academy, and his writings show him to have been a charming and witty man.

It is uncertain when Plato's long career as an author began, but some of his works were probably written not long after Socrates' death. The *Apology*, which purports to relate Socrates' defense of himself in court, seems most likely to have been composed soon after the event. Apart from the *Apology* (an **apology** that seems unrecognizable from what we consider an apology today) and a few letters, everything that we have of Plato's is in the form of dialogues. There are approximately thirty genuine works.

Most of the dialogues fall naturally into three groups: the Socratic dialogues, the political "treatises," and investigations of a wide range of logical/methodological topics. The Socratic dialogues follow Socrates' practice in both the question-and-answer format and the emphasis on ethics—the definitions of the virtues. Typical dialogues and their topics are *Euthyphro*—piety, *Charmides*—temperance, *Lysis*—friendship, *Meno* and *Protagoras*—virtue, *Laches*—courage, *Hippias Major*—beauty, *Philebus*—good, and *Republic I*—justice. The political works are the *Republic II–X*, the *Statesman*, and the *Laws*. In the *Republic*, Socrates is the main speaker, although his interlocutors are now little more than passive listeners. In the *Statesman*, Socrates appears only briefly to introduce the discussion. In the *Laws* he is entirely absent. Among the logical/methodological dialogues, *Cratylus* discusses the correctness of names, *Euthydemus* fallacious argument and the possibility of falsehood, *Sophist* the nature of not being and the possibility of falsehood, *Theaetetus* truth and knowledge, and *Parmenides* philosophy and dialectic. Several dialogues combine serious investigations of philosophy and its methods with other topics: *Phaedo, Republic V–VII, Symposium, Phaedrus, Statesman, Sophist, Timaeus,* and *Philebus.*

Scholars have expended much energy in efforts to establish the order of composition of the dialogues. From antiquity there is testimony that the *Laws* was unfinished at Plato's death. *Theaetetus* refers to the death of the man after whom the dialogue is named, which is known to have taken place in 369 BCE. Some dialogues are introduced as dramatic sequels of others, suggesting a particular order of composition. Apart from such indicators, scholars have had to rely on the probability of an early date for the *Apology* and on the similarities and differences among the works in respect of format, content, and details of style and vocabulary. Yet despite considerable efforts, there is no consensus of opinion.

The order of composition has seemed important because of its bearing on the question of the development of Plato's thought. The large issue here is whether Plato himself, late in his career, repudiated Platonism—the grand philosophical theory on which his fame chiefly rests. He had in several of his major dialogues, including the *Republic,* proposed a radical distinction between the visible world of concrete things and an invisible but intelligible realm of abstract entities. This has come to be popularly known as the theory of **forms**. Among these abstract entities were the shapes and figures of geometry, the numbers of arithmetic, and the moral characteristics that had been the

The Temple of Apollo on the island of Ortigia, the historical center of Syracuse, which Plato visited twice in an attempt to turn the king into a philosopher.

subjects of Socrates' conversations. The scholars who are sometimes called **Trinitarians** have held that Plato came to doubt, and eventually to abandon, his theory. By contrast, the **Unitarians** suppose that Plato acquired a general philosophical orientation from Socrates and maintained it throughout his career, with only augmentation and minor revision along the way.

Plato's nephew, Speusippus, took over the duties of the Academy upon Plato's death. The Academy endured for about 900 years after its founding.

The work of teaching and writing that Plato undertook at the Academy was twice interrupted by ill-fated efforts to realize the ideal of his *Republic* by bringing about rule by a philosopher-king. Twice he traveled to Sicily to educate the young tyrant Dionysius II, who had succeeded his father, Dionysius I. Plato's friend Dion convinced him that the young man, who was Dion's nephew, had the ability and the interest to become a philosopher, thereby uniting wisdom with power. This, Plato had been convinced, was the only salvation for a state. However, the journey ended badly, with jealousy and hard feelings on Dionysius's part, the exile of Dion, and disappointment for Plato.

Several years later, at Dionysius's request, Plato traveled once more to Sicily. This visit ended in a complete breach and led eventually to civil war between Dion's and

Dionysius's forces. Plato returned to the Academy and made no further direct efforts at political reform.

At Plato's death, direction of the Academy passed to the mathematician Speusippus, Plato's nephew. The institution continued as a center of higher education and research until it was closed on the order of the Christian emperor Justinian in 529 CE, approximately 900 years after its founding. As part of his program of violent enforcement of Christian orthodoxy, Justinian issued an edict declaring: "Henceforth never again shall anyone lecture on philosophy or explain the laws in Athens." Some members of the Academy reconstituted themselves in exile, in Persia and then in the **Arab** Middle East. This **rump** Academy persisted until medieval times.

Almost nothing is known of Plato's end, but Diogenes Laertius provides a curious final note. He records what purports to be Plato's will, in which some real property, items of silverware, and a sum of money are bequeathed to "the boy" (his son?), Adeimantus. There are no other suggestions that Plato married, or fathered children.

Over the following pages, Plato engages in an imaginary conversation covering fourteen themes, responding freely to searching questions.

2

THE MAKING OF A PHILOSOPHER

Even as a youth, Plato possessed the immense literary talent that his later work would go on so abundantly to prove. He was, moreover, a **scion** of two wealthy and politically powerful families. He could therefore have looked forward to successful parallel careers as a poet and dramatist, and as a political leader. However, influenced by the example of Socrates' practice (and by that philosopher's fate at the hands of his fellow citizens), young Plato turned his back on both professions and turned to philosophy.

Q. You were a member of a prominent, politically powerful family, presumably marked for a career in politics, and you are clearly a talented writer. What led you to become a philosopher, rather than a politician or a poet?

That's easy: I came to know Socrates. I was a teenaged member of the aristocracy, and here was this squat and rather unattractive son of a stonecutter and a midwife, frequenting the marketplace, the streets, and the homes of the rich and famous, and confounding all the great men by cleverly cross-examining them. Those public men, politicians, poets, and orators hazarded opinions about the nature of virtue, justice, courage, beauty, and the like, but he showed them to have

Socrates reproaching the young Alcibiades for his dissolute lifestyle. Socrates inquired about the nature of virtue.

no real understanding of these things. Socrates proved to us that though it's easy to make claims about these matters, it's very difficult to provide for these claims a basis that will withstand examination. I, as well as two generations of other privileged young men, came to admire Socrates enormously, and some of us were moved to take up his pursuit of this kind of wisdom. Other philosophers, such as Parmenides, Cratylus, and Pythagoras, piqued my interest, but it was getting to know Socrates that changed my life.

Q. This matter of your relation to Socrates is something I'd like to hear a lot more about ... but wasn't it hard for you to turn your back on public life and abandon what must have seemed a promising political career?

Yes, that was difficult. Of course, I wanted very much to take part in leading Athens to a better future. My family and party affiliations made my decision especially painful. Athenians were divided into two parties, the aristocrats and the democrats. During the earliest years of the war, the city was governed by the democrats. After the Athenian defeat by the Spartans, a group of thirty members of the aristocracy was established in power. Their rule was a reign of terror, marked by widespread "legalized" killing. Although I was of their party, and had personal connections to some of them, I was relieved to see them replaced by the restored democracy—a relief that turned to dismay when the democracy put Socrates to death. Like many others, I thought him to have been, of all those of his time, the best, the wisest, and the most righteous.

I saw all of this in my own city, and similarly bad government in other cities. It seemed to me that humankind would never be free from evils until either true philosophers attained political supremacy, or else those who had power became, by some divine intervention, true philosophers. Having at that point no clear idea how to promote these changes, I held back from politics. After a time, I turned my attention to those philosophical inquiries that had occupied Socrates during the happy years when he'd been my friend.

Q. Your admiration of Socrates is evident—just what was it about him that so impressed you?

It wasn't just one single thing, of course. At first I suppose it was the spectacle of this unimposing little man humbling in debate the great and the famous. He surpassed both the great of our city and visitors from other Greek cities, many of whom were renowned for their wisdom and their skill in debate. There was also his manner in discussion—an assumed modesty that left the vanquished refuted not by him but by their own words.

It was his method of question and answer—dialectic, as I call it—that was his greatest gift to me and to philosophy. At first this can seem purely negative, a method of refutation that defeats but doesn't educate. And indeed that's how it was regarded by Socrates' enemies. Yet it became clear to me that this method had a profound significance. It showed that real knowledge was possible in matters where nearly everyone seemed to think there could be nothing more than unsupported opinion.

Q. What matters, for example?

First, those that Socrates was always asking about—the nature of virtue, of justice, of beauty, love, friendship, and the like. I later realized that this applied equally to a range of other matters, such as truth, knowledge, causation, space, time, and reality itself.

Q. And what was this widespread skepticism that you refer to?

You may be so fortunate as to live in a time and place where this **skepticism**, or relativism, is unknown, but in Greece in my time it was **pandemic**. Leading exponents were the sophists, itinerant teachers of rhetoric who, for a fee, taught the art of persuasion without regard to truth. The most philosophical was Protagoras, who provided a theoretical justification for the popular skepticism. His slogan, "Man is the measure of all things," denied there was any objective truth. According to him, there's nothing but opinions—no one of which is any more true than any other. Socrates' practice showed this to be quite wrong.

Q. How? As I understand it, Socrates' method seemed to involve cross-examining people to the point of self-contradiction. How could leaving them confused and perplexed demonstrate the possibility of knowledge? Please explain.

An example from the *Republic* will help to illustrate this. Socrates elicits from Cephalus an opinion as to the nature of justice—that it's telling the truth and returning, or repaying, what one has received. When asked whether returning a borrowed weapon to a man who has lost his mind is just, Cephalus sees—he knows—that it is not, and that his original opinion was wrong. This is the pattern of the Socratic refutations. The respondent is asked a general question as to the nature of something. When he answers, he's then asked a question, or questions, to which he knows the answer. His answers eventually contradict his first opinion, thereby proving it to be false.

Q. Isn't that a pretty insignificant bit of knowledge, though—that justice is not what Cephalus thought it was?

By itself it is, for one purpose, not very significant. However, for another purpose it's all-important. If what one is interested in is the nature of justice, then knowing that justice isn't just telling the truth and returning what one has received doesn't amount to much of an advance, though it's a small step forward. But if one is to assess an extreme subjectivist doctrine such as Protagoras', which man is the measure of all things, then the discovery of any objective, known fact is all-important. It's a fundamental logical principle that a single counter-example refutes a universal proposition. This principle must be understood by anyone who wants to reason about anything.

3

LEARNING THROUGH DIALOGUE

E mulating his revered teacher, Socrates, Plato wrote nearly all of his work in the form of dialogues. Many of his writings closely resemble the kind of conversations that Socrates had actually conducted. Most previous Greek authors had presented positive doctrines that they held to be true, and proclaimed themselves to be deserving of much credit for their discoveries. By contrast, Plato, as author, stands aloof and never speaks on his own behalf. The words of his characters are left to stand or fall on their own.

Q. Except for a few letters, everything you wrote is in the form of dialogues. Why did you leave us nothing but these conversations?

It's pretty obvious, I'd have thought, that I aimed to achieve in writing the same effect that Socrates had in his conversations. My earliest works were consciously modeled on the actual conversations of Socrates. What you really want to know is why I thought this form the most appropriate to my own purposes. My overall intention was to promote understanding in philosophy. I hesitate to call this teaching, because that suggests I was trying to put something into the minds of the learners—which is quite the wrong idea of what constitutes real education. Worthwhile learning is really a drawing out from the mind of the learner, rather than a putting in. Socrates famously denied that he ever taught, instead insisting that he'd followed in the footsteps of his midwife mother. Just as she'd helped young women to give birth to babies, he simply helped young men to give birth to ideas. By questioning them, he simply drew forth from them knowledge that was already in them. Socrates' success seems to me adequate proof that learning, at least in philosophy, really is based on knowledge that is somehow already possessed by the learner. Since I viewed education as Socrates had, it was natural that I should try to emulate in my writing his oral "teaching."

Q. Who are we to take to be speaking for you in these dialogues?

What is written in the dialogues is what those characters have to say. It may or may not reflect the opinions of the actual persons whose names the characters bear. In assessing what the characters say, keep in mind that their statements may be offered only as suggestions to be considered. Myths, metaphors, allegories, and images are obviously not to be taken literally. Furthermore, the words of the leading characters may or may not represent my own opinions. These are imagined conversations that I take to be philosophically interesting. My aim in writing them is to stimulate philosophical reasoning. Beyond that, I take no responsibility for what any of my characters has to say.

Socrates was troubled by apparent disagreements among the Greek gods over what was pious and not pious, and what was pleasing and not pleasing.

Q. But if you withdraw so far from your written words, won't it be impossible for the reader to know your true opinions?

Now you're beginning to get the point. In philosophy, you see, learning is not gathering up opinions. It's reasoning— thinking things through. If I give you my opinion, what have I given you? Even if it's correct, you have nothing of value if you haven't earned it by reasoning it through. Without the understanding of why it must be so, you have no real knowledge. For example, take something I'm entirely certain of—the Pythagorean theorem in geometry. I can tell you that the square on the hypotenuse of a right-angled triangle is equal to the sum of the squares on the other two sides. No doubt you'll believe this. However, unless you've thought out for yourself the fairly elaborate reasoning that proves it, all you have is a flimsy opinion, rather than secure knowledge. In philosophy, most of the propositions that we entertain are by no means as certain as geometrical theorems. It's imperative that we treat every proposition as a hypothesis to be subjected to the kind of scrutiny we've learned from Socrates.

Q. Then how are we to conduct this conversation? Will you really pretend that nothing you've written is your own opinion?

No, I won't do that. We're here in private conversation, and the subject is, I gather, myself. So I'll answer questions as to what I believe, and I'll grant that much of what I put into the mouths of my characters is my own opinion. But, you know, the shoe would be on the other foot if you were to converse with Socrates, or if you entered the Academy as a student. You'd then be answering questions, rather than asking them. And your answers would be fitted one against another, with the true ones displacing the false. Still, I won't disown my opinions here. You may assume that I do believe the opinions to which the dialogues seem to point. If the assumption is wrong, I'll correct you. The one proviso I do insist on is that my opinions are, like everyone else's, to be treated as hypotheses. I really do acknowledge the danger that I'm wrong, and intend nothing I say to be immune to scrutiny.

Q. That's a relief, but I still have one misgiving about your dialectic. You grant that its success depends on the learner's already having knowledge of the subject. How can we undertake to learn what we already know?

Yes, that does sound paradoxical, but think about this analogous example. Suppose you've forgotten the name of an acquaintance and need to recall it—perhaps you're approaching him in the hallway and want to greet him by name. As he comes nearer, you have it, you think, and you greet him confidently: "Good morning, Callicles." Two steps later it strikes you: "Brother, it's Cratylus!" Here you thought you knew, but you were wrong. Yet somehow the knowledge *was* within you, because when his actual name came to you, you recognized it. What we claim for dialectic is like this. Though you'll probably get it wrong when you try to say what holiness or justice or beauty is, you have in you somehow the knowledge of these things. This is proved by the fact that when you're asked the right questions, you're able to answer them correctly.

4

THE PRIMACY OF THE GOOD

Nearly everyone at some point faces the question, *What constitutes the good life?* Some answer that the good in life is pleasure, others that it is observance of duties and obligations, still others that it is obedience to divine commands. Against all these, Socrates had contended that what makes our life good is just being a good person—a virtuous person. Plato agreed, though he struggled to find a convincing justification for the idea.

Q. You have quite a lot to say about the good. What do you think that is?

Actually, it's a little easier to say what it isn't. First, it isn't pleasure, because pleasure, if it's taken in something wicked or cruel, is a bad thing. And neither can it be, as we philosophers are sometimes inclined to think, knowledge. There is much knowledge that's trivial or useless. So the good must be something else.

Q. That doesn't seem so hard. Isn't it just happiness?

Well, that's the easy answer, and I guess it isn't wrong. But it doesn't take us very far. We're still left with the question of what constitutes happiness. We still have to consider the

Depicted here, Socrates drinks the poison hemlock. Socrates was condemned to death on charges of impiety and corrupting the young.

same candidates—pleasure, satisfaction, self-realization, and so on. None of these seems right because we can imagine a person having achieved any of these and yet living a life that no one would want.

Q. Why do you say that no one would want a life filled with pleasure? To many of us that sounds awfully good.

OK, let's face this head on. Let's imagine a life filled with every supposed benefit we can imagine save one—moral virtue. To make this vivid, I'll ask you to suspend your disbelief and suppose that I'm an extraordinarily powerful sorcerer and that I have, moreover, the capacity to arrange the entire world to suit my fancy. Now, I'll make you an offer. If you'll permit me to transform you into a thoroughly wicked person, then I'll grant you everything else that you wish. You may be as wealthy as you please, you may marry or otherwise consort with whom you please, you may have a reputation as a great and honorable person, and whatever else pleases you.

Q. That sounds pretty good, except for one thing— my conscience would make me miserable if I were to behave miserably. Can you fix this for me, too?

Yes, I can even tweak your conscience. You'll be a scoundrel, but you'll never know it. You'll think as well of yourself as everyone else does. All you have to do is sign the permission slip for me to perform the transformation, and you'll wake up to the blessed life of the villain without a conscience. I see you cringe, and your hand trembles as you contemplate that fateful signature. I'm sure that neither you nor any other self-respecting person would make that bargain. One's own good character is the most precious thing in life. I saw in Socrates a man who led the best of lives, though he endured much hardship and died unjustly condemned. He said, and I believed, that not he but the Athenians themselves were the victims of their unjust verdict.

Q. That's all very well, but surely you wouldn't say that if Socrates had lived his entire life wracked with pain, had had no friends, and had seen his sons grow into vicious criminals, he would still have lived happily and well. Would you?

I hesitate a little there. It may be that some of what we usually regard as great goods are necessary as preconditions for the happy life. But I think that they're not the essence of it. Being upright, honest, wise, and courageous are the essence of the happy life. My take on the good life can be summed up in a few words: Virtue is its own reward.

Q. You're not alone in saying this, but I suspect that you really mean it in a way that others don't. What consequence does this have for us all?

For us in our individual lives the consequence is pretty obvious—we should live so that we nurture in our souls those human virtues that we admire.

For our communal life—our life as a community—this implies that we should so organize our states as to maximize the growth of virtue in all our citizens, since that's the essence of their well-being.

5

THE PRICE OF WRONGDOING

I n human conduct we are all too familiar with voluntary wrongdoing—doing something wrong while being well aware that it is wrong. This is our whole basis for the reproach and punishment of wrongdoers. We suppose that our motives to do right are sometimes overcome by stronger desires to do something that is wrong. Socrates and Plato challenged this commonsense view, contending that, appearances notwithstanding, no one does wrong willingly.

Q. You've said that no one ever does wrong willingly. What did you mean by that?

It might be a little more accurate to say that no one ever does wrong *knowingly*. One would never do a thing knowing it to be wrong.

Q. All right, I know what you're saying, but what makes you think that it's true?

Just as the greatest good for a person is to be a good person, so the greatest evil must be to be an evil person. To do wrong is to make oneself a worse person. So to do wrong knowingly would be to bring the worst harm upon oneself. Since no one would knowingly bring harm upon himself, or herself, it

King David Handing the Letter to Uriah, a painting that shows the Hebrew leader sending the husband of his lover off to certain death in battle.

follows that no one would knowingly do wrong.

Q. That argument has a ring of plausibility about it, but isn't it overcome by the plain facts of experience? You may know of the Jewish king, David, who because he coveted the wife of one of his soldiers, sent the soldier into battle where he was sure to be killed. Surely you admit that the king wronged this man?

For the sake of the argument, yes, I'll grant that the king wronged the soldier.

Q. And he did this knowing that it was wrong?

Yes, but he did it out of ignorance. He did it from his lack of awareness of what he was doing. Under the influence of a mindless impulse he was blinded to the true nature of his action. By acting so he was making himself to be a person whom anyone, including himself, must hold in contempt. Your knowledge of this shows that his infamy has outlived him by thousands of years! What person of sound mind would accept that in exchange for the companionship of a mate, however attractive he or she might be?

Q. You make it sound as if the ill fame that he earned was the price that King David paid for his wickedness. Would he have fared better if no one had known of his treachery?

No, not at all. I meant it when I said that it's our moral character, more than our reputation, that counts. By his treachery your king blackened his soul. And he would have been no less wretched if he hadn't been found out. Had he thought sufficiently about the cost to himself of being a murderer he would never have accepted that burden in exchange for the pleasure of the woman's company. The ignorance that he suffered was not of the wrongness of his action, but of the inevitable cost to himself of being so debased. Just as virtue is its own reward, so wickedness is its own punishment.

6

DEMOCRACY AND PHILOSOPHER-KINGS

I n the West, we now regard democracy as the best form of government, a judgment that we base on considerations of fairness and individual rights. We believe that it would be unfair to deprive any citizen of the right to have a say in the government of the state. Plato seemed to disagree with us with regard to the best form of government and the basis for the choice. In his *Republic*, he seemed to rate democracy as vastly inferior to rule by philosophers, although in the *Laws* he gave a different impression.

Q. You certainly raised some hackles when in the *Republic* you rated democracy as the next to worst form of government, inferior even to military dictatorship or rule by the wealthy few, and superior only to tyranny. Do you really think it's that bad?

Yes—but perhaps we should make clear what sort of democracy I was considering. We might call it direct, or pure, democracy, in which the citizens are empowered to determine public policy by majority vote. Decisions regarding war and peace, as well as all lesser matters, are left to the judgment of the people.

Italian dictator Benito Mussolini is an example of a demagogue acclaimed by the people who turned into a tyrant. This lithograph was published in an Italian newspaper in 1934.

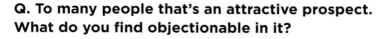

Q. To many people that's an attractive prospect. What do you find objectionable in it?

Attractive it is—in theory. The freedom and sense of autonomy that it offers have undeniable appeal. People have a natural desire to feel empowered, and this form of government offers that empowerment. However, in direct democracy the price is too high. Wise decision-making requires a great deal of knowledge, careful deliberation, and a profound understanding of the proper aims of government. Where the mere desires of the majority of citizens are supreme, these attributes have no place. Thoughtless and foolish decisions are as likely to be made as wise and prudent ones.

This sort of democracy also carries within it the seeds of decline into the worst of governments—tyranny. If each citizen feels free to follow his own impulses, factions and discord are almost bound to erupt. Where this becomes bitter, a **demagogue** who fashions himself "champion of the people" is likely to arise, to surround himself with bodyguards to protect him from "enemies of the people," and eventually to seize tyrannical control of the state.

Like aristocracy, **oligarchy**, and monarchy, democracy seems to me less a real **polity** than an enslavement of the state by one or another of its parts, be it the well-born, the wealthy, kings, or the majority of the citizens.

Q. So what do you recommend? And what were you getting at when you indicated that what you condemned was just one form of democracy?

Taking into account the tendency of unrestrained power to corrupt those who wield it, I came to favor a mixed polity,

Plato believed that ruling powers and magistrates should be subservient to the law.

as I said in the *Statesman* and the *Laws*—one that combines some features of monarchy and some of democracy. There must be some whose task it is to administer the laws, but their power must not be exercised without the constraint of law and the consent of the people. By far the most important feature of our polity is the supremacy of the laws. Wherever the law is subservient and impotent, over that state I see ruin impending. But wherever the law is lord over the magistrates, and the magistrates are servants to the law, there I see salvation and all the blessings that the gods bestow on states. To ensure the subservience of the magistrates to the law, there must be a clear division of power among them. They must be elected for fixed terms by their fellow citizens, and they must all be liable to indictment for misdemeanors during their terms in office and careful audits at the end of their terms—with severe penalties for malfeasance. In order for this polity to succeed, the state must be small enough that the electors can know who among them is best suited to govern, and the state must adopt public education as its first priority. I'm convinced that if the task of educating the citizens is well carried out, then everything will work out, and if it isn't, then nothing can save the day. If you like, you can call this polity "representative constitutional democracy."

Q. Now I'm really confused. I take your point that one can usefully distinguish direct from representative democracy, but didn't you in your *Republic* present aristocracy, the rule of philosopher-kings, as the ideal form of government? What changed your mind?

You're right about the philosopher-kings, but wrong about the change of mind. In the *Laws*, the idea was to imagine a constitution for a proposed new state on the island of Crete. The task was the practical one of outlining a feasible polity, taking into account all the facts of geography and of human psychology. In the *Republic* the task was entirely different. The topic there was justice. Socrates, in order best to discern the nature of justice, imagined a perfect state, in which the tasks of government were carried out by philosophers without the constraints of law or popular election—a state that would embody the virtue of justice. In contriving this ideal it seemed to me not to matter whether it was actually feasible.

The desirability of this form of government, of course, depends on the philosophers being both perfectly wise and entirely incorruptible. If we could count on always finding such paragons, this form of rule would be superior to one in which general laws were supreme. But human beings are such that this, though not impossible, is unlikely. In the end I recommend a second best to the ideal—one in which the law would stand proxy for philosophy, producing in the state a balance of freedom and friendship that seems to me to have been best achieved in the ancient Athens of my remote ancestors.

7

FREEDOM AND CENSORSHIP

Freedom of speech, freedom of artistic expression, and freedom to travel are now regarded as universal human rights. Their infringement, except in the most extraordinary circumstances, is regarded as a crime. Ignoring all questions of individual rights, and taking into account only the good of society, Plato recommended severe restrictions on all of these freedoms. Banishment and even death were prescribed for violations. Nonetheless, he considered a certain degree of freedom of speech to be essential to good government.

Q. In 1945, a widely read 20th-century writer published a book titled *The Open Society and its Enemies*. Guess who's the leading enemy! The author, Karl Popper, was a refugee from the German tyrant Adolf Hitler, and he cast you as the first Hitlerite. Is it fair to characterize you as an enemy of the open society?

I guess that depends a lot on what the open society is open to. No doubt I recommended more restrictions on what people should be exposed to than many think necessary, though I suspect that nearly everyone will admit the need for some restrictions. Perhaps you can make up your

Stories highlighting lack of self-control by Zeus were viewed by Plato as a bad example for children.

47

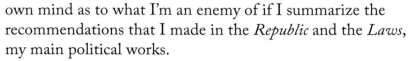

own mind as to what I'm an enemy of if I summarize the recommendations that I made in the *Republic* and the *Laws*, my main political works.

Let's begin with the limitations on the experience of children. Children are greatly influenced by the stories they're told, the games they play, the dances they dance, and the music they hear. Since character is so much determined in childhood, it's important that we bring to bear the good influences and relieve our children of the burden of the bad.

Tales, then, of wickedness among the gods or of unpunished villainy among humans must be censored. No good can come of giving a wayward youth the excuse that Zeus himself behaves with utter lack of self-control. Role-playing also should be limited to the imitation of the courageous and the just. There are dances and music that tend to create frenzy or, conversely, softness in the soul. These too must be dismissed in favor of dancing and music that promote order and strength. All of this seems to me necessary to set children on the right path.

Q. I don't know whether many of us would go quite as far as you recommend, but we do recognize the need to limit the exposure of our children to harmful influences. But surely you'll relax the limitations on adults, won't you?

Not as much as you may think. Every action of government is justified only by its tendency to promote the well-being of the citizens, and that well-being consists, so I maintain, in their being as good and virtuous as they can be. Therefore, the proper actions of government will all have as their aim nothing other than promoting the virtue of the citizens.

Dramatists may have contributed to the death of Socrates. William Blake Richmond's *An Audience in Athens during Agememnon by Aeschylus* depicts the auditorium of the theater at Athens.

This duty of government is just as valid toward adults as toward children. Even adults must be protected from corrupting influences.

Q. This talk of corrupting influences reminds me of the charge against Socrates—that he corrupted the young. Aren't you in danger of regulation that would have outlawed your own hero?

I don't think so. What I would forbid is, in nearly every case, falsehood. The banned influences are either in themselves false or they tend to promote falsehood in the souls of those they affect. Socrates' actions were quite the opposite of these. As far as a human is capable of doing so, he promoted truth and knowledge, not falsehood and error.

Q. Well, your principles sound noble, but who's qualified to act as censor?

Censorship will, of course, be left to state officials. In matters of religion, distinguished priests and educators will have to act as censors. While in the regulation of foreign travel, who acts as censor will depend on the travel's purpose. This regulatory function of government is one that I've always taken seriously, and it's important that there be rigid safeguards against its abuse. I took some pains to lay out details in the *Laws*.

Q. Can you give us an idea of what the corrupting influences are, and how you'd combat them?

First, I suppose, are the poets and dramatists. Poets have represented gods behaving terribly and humans faring well despite their wickedness. Such stories fail to satisfy both the tests for censorship—they are false and they promote bad character and bad behavior. The harm that dramatists can do is illustrated by Aristophanes' comedy *The Clouds*. In this parody, Socrates is represented as an unscrupulous sophist, able to make the weaker argument appear the stronger. He teaches this skill to a throng of disciples. This false portrayal probably influenced Socrates' conviction. Dramatists are so prone to portray human weakness and folly that they cannot serve a useful purpose in an enlightened society.

So, although it's with a heavy heart, I recommend that all imitative artists be banned from the state. And yet, if it can be shown that their works are beneficial to society, then they'll be welcomed back and garlands will be placed on their heads.

Another influence that must be quelled is that of the atheists. Those who deny the existence of the gods are probably as great a danger to good order as those who represent the gods as immoral. The proper first response is to educate these people. They should be imprisoned and visited at midnight by a "Nocturnal Council" of the city's most distinguished philosophers. The Council would reason with the atheists, aiming to prove to them the error of their opinion. If this fails—if they're **intransigent** in their unbelief—then they should be given a choice. Either they'll agree to keep their opinions to themselves or they'll be put to death and their bodies thrown over the walls of the city for the wolves.

Q. Now you're making my hair stand on end! Capital punishment for unbelief? Do you realize that if you carried out this policy in the 21st century, you'd be killing most philosophers, your own people?

The punishment is not for unbelief alone—atheists who'll be quiet will be allowed their freedom. I admit that the punishment for those who proselytize may seem harsh. I've insisted that the only proper motive for punishment is to make the miscreant better. But in the case of our unrestrained atheists there's no way to make them better, since they resist re-education. So the only improvement is to make them less wretched by ending their miserable lives.

Your suggestion that most philosophers are atheists is almost unbelievable. To me it seems pretty clear that the order we can plainly see in the universe calls for some explanation. And the only credible explanation I can think of is some sort of divine creation. If generations of philosophers have come to believe otherwise, then I'm rather at a loss. Of course, I'm not eager to kill these people. This must surely be

Freedom of speech was seen as contributing to the public good in debates over government policy. However, Socrates' support of censorship contradicts this.

one of those occasions on which we can all benefit from a careful dialogue. We should all—and that includes myself— be willing to subject our opinions to scrutiny. Really, I would rather talk to these people than kill them.

Q. That's a conversation I'd certainly like to hear. But back to the influences from which you propose to save even adults. Are there others besides artists and atheists?

Yes—foreigners. I recommended in the *Laws* that the new city planned for Crete should be sited about ten miles from the sea. Seaports promote intercourse with foreigners, both by bringing them to the port and by encouraging travel to foreign lands. Citizens who are too easily influenced may emulate foreign ways without understanding their drawbacks. Only citizens who are both of impeccable character and highly educated should be allowed access to foreign societies.

Q. You've proposed heavy restrictions. Is there to be no freedom of expression in your state?

Yes, some freedoms are vitally important. Our aim is to promote well-being in our society. This requires that we do everything we can to increase wisdom and knowledge. So, where we rely on election of our government officials, we must make provision that every citizen be entirely free to speak in debates about government policies. Elected officials have no monopoly on wisdom, and they must be allowed to benefit from the counsel of their compatriots. Also, the inhabitants of our own city may have something to learn from other cities. So it's important that those of our citizens who are capable of judging these things should experience the ways of others. Freedom of expression and freedom of inquiry are both important, but only to the extent that they're likely to be beneficial to the society.

So, to return to your question about me and the open society, I say that society should be open to influences that are good and closed to those that are bad. It's the task of the lawgiver to design institutions and mechanisms that are capable of distinguishing the one from the other.

8

ON WOMEN'S EQUALITY

Plato was a pioneer in advocating the equality of women. In his time this proposal was vastly more controversial than it is now, at least in many parts of the world. Since women were almost completely excluded from many occupations and civic activities, their abilities could not be proven as they are at present, when women actually do the things that men alone were once thought capable of doing. Plato had, therefore, to find another way of justifying his proposal.

Q. You've mentioned the exclusion of women from the intellectual life of your community, and we know that you championed the equality of women. Just what did you recommend and why?

I recommended for women what I recommended for everyone. Each person should enjoy privileges and rewards solely on the basis of his or her abilities and character. No one should ever enjoy preferment over anyone else on the basis of wealth or family connection or any feature unconnected to merit.

Plato held radically different views from his contemporaries on the role of women.

Q. That's a fine principle, but how did it lead you to advocate women's equality? After all, the principle still doesn't declare women to be equally meritorious.

I realize that, but the justification for my proposals isn't that hard to find. What I recommended is that women be given the same education and the same vocational opportunities as men, along with equal citizenship. No preferences and no disabilities. Where necessary for their work, women should be relieved even of the burdens of childcare. What's needed to justify this is only to show that it's not somehow impossible or contrary to nature, and that it would be for the best. The possibility of women doing the same work as men can be shown by a simple analogy. Humans are animals, and the difference between male and female humans is like the difference between males and females of other animal species. With animals no

Work, in Plato's view, should be assigned by ability and not by gender.

one is so mad as to say that the mare is unsuited to carrying a rider or pulling a wagon, or that the bitch is unsuited to guarding the sheep. Therefore, the difference between male and female humans does not disqualify the females from the work that the males have done.

Q. I have a feeling that some women won't be pleased at being classed as animals, even in so good a cause as this.

I'm sorry, but it's really just a plain biological fact. If it will help to soothe feelings, I'm happy to note that men are as much animals as women are.

Q. I'm not sure how soothing that will be! Anyway, I have another misgiving about your rationale for the equality of women. Why did you not appeal to the innate human right of women to equal treatment?

I won't disparage ethical reasoning based on claims to individual rights. That may have some use in settling some moral issues. But my practice is always to look to human well-being, to look to the good. So far, it hasn't seemed necessary to look elsewhere. If it turns out that my way of thinking leads us astray, then there'll surely be reason enough to seek other grounds for our moral judgments.

Q. Okay, you've shown the equal treatment of women not to be contrary to nature, but might it not be contrary to good public policy? Might not the social costs, primarily to the family, outweigh the benefits?

When we're weighing things like this, we have to rely on probabilities. But there are a couple of things I'm pretty

Gender roles are reversed on this painting of an Amazon, warrior circa 470 BCE.

sure of. The good of the society is ultimately the well-being of its members. I've already argued that the well-being of a person is just being good—achieving human excellence. So it must be the aim of a well-governed state to enable as many of its members as possible to reach their full potential. To exclude a full half of the population from this is to deny society a priceless benefit. Another factor, though a less important one, is the practical loss of women's intellectual contributions. It seems highly likely that if women continue to be repressed, then important positions will

Didrachm of Amastris, who was the first woman to issue coins in her own name, circa 285 BCE.

be held by people of lesser ability. This constitutes a loss to society—a greater loss, I think, than would be incurred by freeing some women from the task of tending the family.

Q. You believe that, but isn't it an empirical question, which can finally be settled only by an actual test?

Yes, of course. But I think you're playing with an old man here. Unless I've got it all wrong, your own society is trying this very experiment. I never had your opportunity to judge because during my time people were unwilling to try out my proposals. I never thought it would be centuries, let alone millennia, before there would be a serious trial of them.

9

PLATONIC LOVE

Erotic love is ordinarily taken to be just the familiar sexual impulse. Yet in the *Symposium*, Plato has Socrates praise *eros* as something that rises far above and beyond sex. In its highest manifestation, it is said to be grasped only by those who have advanced far in philosophy. Eros has a place for homosexual love and is related to friendship, or *philia*. Despite the elevation of love to a highly intellectual level in Socrates' speech, Plato acknowledges the more familiar aspects of it in the speeches of Aristophanes and other participants in the *Symposium*.

Q. You've had a lot to say about love, and we're familiar with the term "Platonic love." To us that suggests some vaguely asexual or non-sexual affection. Is that really what you had in mind?

Not at all. You mean what we called philia, something like brotherly love. You're doubtless familiar with such terms as "philately," "philanthropy," and "bibliophile." These are all genuinely asexual, but they're not what I was most interested in. What I was really thinking of was eros. I imagine your society is quite familiar with the erotic. Well, what I was thinking of was that very thing, but apprehended in its true light rather

Love, illustrated as *Cupid in a Tree*, is elevated beyond a desire to possess.

than just in its lowest manifestation. Rather than asexual or nonsexual, you might say it's hypersexual or meta-sexual.

Q. Whoa! What are you saying—that Platonic love is plain old lust, just ratcheted up into something more intense and frenzied?

Very funny, my friend! But I'm sure you know I didn't mean that. Love, properly understood, is indeed something beyond the familiar urge that you call lust. But it goes beyond such urges not by becoming more intense but rather by being enlarged and elevated.

Q. Enlarged? How?

Well, the familiar erotic arousal is directed toward a physical body, the body of a youth or a woman. From this, one who advances in love may progress to the love of a beautiful soul. And this love of an individual body or soul will, in turn, be generalized to a love of all beautiful bodies and all beautiful souls. The next advance will be to cherishing the beauty in shared culture, institutions, and laws. The person who's advanced this far will have considerably enlarged the scope of the beloved—and will consequently have experienced a diminished ardor for beautiful bodies.

Q. Wait. Isn't erotic love specific to an individual body or soul? How can love of bodies generally, let alone love of practices and institutions, be the same thing?

What seems to me the essential feature of erotic love is that it's a species of desire. Specifically, *it's a desire to possess that which is beloved.* When we keep that in mind, it's not so hard to see the generalized affection for the beautiful to be of the same kind as that intense sexual desire we're so familiar with. Perhaps you'd more easily recognize the generalization I have in mind if you thought of it as a transference, or sublimation, of sexual desire.

Q. Well, is that what it is, then?

No, there are a couple more steps on the path to true love. Beyond the appreciation of beautiful laws and practices lies an infatuation with all branches of knowledge. This culminates in the love of wisdom—philosophy. And, at last, one who has become enamored of philosophy will come to possess, intellectually, the very nature of beauty itself. This is the final climactic stage of love.

Q. Beauty itself! What is that, and what exactly do you mean by possession of it?

Beauty is one of those things that's really understood only after a very long and arduous inquiry. This much, though, is certain—that it's something good. Because it's good, it's desirable. By that I mean that it's worthy of desire. So its presence in something makes that thing itself worthy of love.

Beyond this I don't want to commit myself. In one of the dialogues Socrates suggested that beauty was something comparative. A beautiful pot would be ugly by comparison with a beautiful maiden, and the maiden would suffer when compared with a goddess. Whether this is so, or whether beauty is something absolute, is a matter on which I won't pronounce. Like the other natures that matter most to us, such as truth and justice, beauty remains to be fully revealed.

What I meant by the possession of the nature of beauty is the complete understanding of it that I've just mentioned. The grasp of beauty itself is one of the most prized achievements of dialectic.

Q. I can see how your Platonic love is enlarged beyond sexual love, and elevated above it, but I'm a little confused as to how this is distinguished from philia. You've implied that philosophy is erotic, whereas philanthropy is not. How come?

We can say in a word what distinguishes eros from philia—desire. As I've mentioned, by its very nature eros *is* desire. Compare that with philanthropy. When you love your darling, you desire that person to be yours—but your love of humankind does not wish it to be yours. The philanthropic impulse is an urge to give rather than to get. Philia and eros share the fact that they are both affections, but they're dissimilar in that eros is a possessive urge.

I understand why you should be puzzled about philosophy. The similar prefixes suggest that it and philanthropy are both species of philia. All I can say is that I'm not responsible for the implications of our language.

Q. You present homosexual love as a perfectly natural affection. Yet even today some faiths and societies view homosexuality as unnatural. What do we need to understand here?

First, I suppose, you need to wake up to the fact that homosexual impulses do occur in humans, even in the very best of our species. I offer my own brother, Glaucon, as one of the most ardent lovers of young men. Beyond that, you have to understand the nature of the society I lived in. Because of the segregation of women on the basis of their roles in society, companionship was pretty much limited to people of the same sex. In my time, men and women would not be mixed in public places. It was natural that intimate relations should develop among men. I never observed relationships among women closely.

Q. And you never found same-sex sex at all troublesome?

You have to be a little careful here. Sex, whether heterosexual or homosexual, can be unseemly or inappropriate. That I do find wrong. I think one should behave temperately and with scrupulous regard for propriety. As in so many things, Socrates here serves as an admirable example. Socrates met my uncle, Charmides, when Charmides was thought to be the most beautiful and most promising young man in Athens. Socrates felt a strong attraction but curbed his primal impulses. Instead, he proceeded to question the young man to discover whether his soul was as beautiful as his body. This exemplifies perfectly the ascent toward what you call **Platonic** love. Note that I don't praise chastity for its own sake. It's valuable as an element in propriety and as an essential step in the broadening and uplifting that leads to true and pure love.

Q. You've said that you were more interested in eros than philia. Why the preference?

I suppose it's partly because of the more dynamic role that it plays in nature and in human affairs. Eros is not only *possessive*, it's also *productive*. It's what impels humans and

other animals to reproduce. Moreover, if we may conjecture about the origins of the world, we may even suppose it to have been the impetus for creation.

Q. Have you nothing good to say for philia?

On the contrary, I say it's as important in our lives as anything can be. Within a community it's absolutely essential. Without this friendly feeling of citizen for citizen, any society would descend into factions and enmity. One wouldn't want everyone in society to have erotic designs on everyone else, but universal friendship would be most desirable. And, within the family, nothing is so important as this amity between husband and wife. Eros has its vital role, but over the long haul it's philia that's the salvation of the family.

Q. This is all very cerebral. Aren't you asking a bit much of your readers to accept your account of erotic love, something that's so much associated with joy, and so little with thought?

Yes, to be sure. This is a philosopher's take on love. It can be viewed from different perspectives—as you'll note that it was in the *Symposium*. There, the celebrants forgo the usual party entertainment and heavy drinking in favor of a conversation in which each tries to outdo the others in praise of eros.

Among them Aristophanes stands out for his display of comedic imagination. Humans, he says, were originally double creatures having two faces and four arms and legs. They walked on four legs as we do on two, but when they got to running, they'd spin, as acrobats do in somersaults. There were three sorts of these original humans. Some

There are many perspectives on love presented in the *Symposium*.

were female on both sides, some were male, and some—the true **hermaphrodites**—were part male, part female. These magnificent creatures were so ambitious that they conspired against the gods. Not wanting to destroy or banish them, Zeus split them in two, leaving them to walk on just two feet. In case the humans were not sufficiently humbled, he reserved the option to split them again and leave them to hop on one foot. The newly divided humans had their cut sides covered with skin pulled tight and tied at the navel.

A Corinthian terraccotta statue from the fourth century BCE depicts
Aphrodite, the Greek goddess of love.

Their heads, limbs, and private parts were moved around to the cut side, and this allowed reproduction in the way that we know. Each divided human strives without knowing it for union with its other half. Those whose whole nature was male delight in the embrace of men, those who were double females desire women, and those who were men-women seek after the opposite sex. This craving for union, and the delight in its achievement, is, says Aristophanes, love.

Q. Fascinating! But what was your purpose in joining this and the other speeches with Socrates' account of love?

In the way that poets can, Aristophanes does here provide some insight into the nature of love. Even the speech of Socrates' old comrade in arms, Alcibiades, helps to complete the picture of love. He enters the party already drunk and unwittingly contributes to the discussion by confessing his infatuation with Socrates. His affection encompasses his admiration of Socrates' bravery in battle (to which he owes his life), the shame that he feels when he compares his own life with that of Socrates, and the appreciation of the splendid restraint with which Socrates resisted his attempt to seduce him.

Q. What you call the philosopher's take on love is presented by Socrates. The other speakers in the *Symposium* offer very different views. Where do you really stand?

With the philosopher, of course. But, though I take back nothing of what I've had Socrates express, I'm happy to let others have their say.

10

MISADVENTURE IN SICILY

T he political theory of the *Republic* called for rule by philosopher-kings. In late middle age, Plato was challenged to travel to Sicily to put his ideal into practice by educating the reigning young tyrant of Syracuse, Dionysius II. Syracuse was known as the most luxurious and debauched of the Greek cities. In his *Seventh Letter,* Plato explains his motives for accepting the challenge—and recounts the outcome of what he himself suspected was a fool's errand.

Q. Though you acknowledge the impracticality of rule by philosopher-kings, you spent a good deal of time and effort trying to transform the young tyrant of Syracuse into that very thing, a philosopher-king. Isn't that a little inconsistent?

No, not really. I always regarded rule by philosophers as the ideal. However, when recommending a polity built from scratch, it seemed to me that the ideal would present too much risk of deterioration into lesser forms of government, even perhaps to tyranny. In Syracuse, though, we weren't starting from scratch, but from an already-entrenched tyranny. So there was room for improvement but not for decline.

There was, moreover, considerable pressure on me personally to at least try to put into practice what I'd preached. On an earlier visit to Syracuse I found in Dion a friend who

In the *Sword of Damocles*, the courtier Damocles takes the seat of the tyrant Dionysius II of Syracuse and discovers that those in power face constant danger.

was enamored of philosophy and who came to share my view of government. When he later assured me that the young Dionysius was a promising candidate, and he and Dionysius himself urged me to come and undertake the young man's education, I found it hard to resist. I resolved to leave my work at the Academy and undertake the task of transforming a tyranny into a true aristocracy.

Q. How did that go? Did the young tyrant live up to your expectations?

It didn't go at all well. Dionysius seemed eager to please me at first, but a couple of things doomed our efforts. One of these was, I confess, my own haste. Since I was assured the youth had made great headway in philosophy, I set out straight away to help him to lay down a set of just laws. This, of course, violated my own principle that a ruler must undergo rigorous training in philosophy before taking on the task of ruling. It also led to the second, overwhelming impediment to our success. Dionysius was surrounded by people who became extremely jealous of Dion and me. They persuaded Dionysius that I favored Dion over him and that Dion was conspiring against him. Their **calumny** succeeded. Dion was exiled, though allowed to retain an income from his properties. I was detained for some time as a "guest."

Eventually I was allowed to leave, on the understanding that I might come back when the time was right. I returned, much relieved, to Athens and the Academy.

Q. That didn't end your involvement in Syracusian politics, though. Why did you make that long trip yet again?

Although I had no desire to return to Sicily, and no confidence that I could reform Dionysius, the man had a strong hold over me. Dion had joined me at the Academy, and he longed to go home and be restored to his family. Dionysius promised that if I'd come and serve as his mentor again, Dion's affairs would be arranged as we wished.

Q. How did you get on the second time around?

Worse even than I'd imagined. This time, I did follow my own advice. I told Dionysius that it was really necessary that he prepare himself for rule by acquiring an education. We began, as I'd always recommended, with rigorous exercises in mathematics. Needless to say, we hadn't got very far before his impatience grew into annoyance.

In the end, the outcome of this second effort was favorable neither to me nor to Dion. Dion's exile was continued, and he lost even the income from his property. I was held as a prisoner, and was in considerable danger of being killed by Dionysius's enemies, who supposed that since I was his "guest," I was also his ally. After some very unpleasant confrontations, some Italian friends sent a ship to Syracuse with an urgent plea that I be allowed to go home. Dionysius agreed, and I was allowed to make my escape.

Q. And what did you learn from all of this?

That question is more than a little impertinent. None of what happened was a surprise to me. I knew from the beginning that the odds against success were long. I might have learned something if things had worked out differently from the way that I expected. There's no easy road to the ideal state, and I knew that all along.

ARISTOTELI STAGIRITAE

11

BRILLIANT MINDS

T here were already in Plato's time schools aimed at advanced education. In Athens, Plato's rival, Isocrates, had a school of rhetoric. In Cyrene, there was a school of mathematics, with the geometer Eudoxus as its central figure. The Pythagorean mathematical/religious community thrived in southern Italy. In a grove dedicated to the hero Hecademus on the outskirts of Athens, Plato built his own school and research center. It quickly rose to preeminence and continued in Athens for 900 years, making it the longest-lasting "university" that the world has so far known, surpassing in longevity even the University of Paris.

Q. You've mentioned your Academy, whose name we still use as the collective name for institutions of higher learning. What moved you to create it?

There were two things on my mind. First, I realized that, after the death of Socrates, young people lacked the opportunity I'd had to learn philosophy firsthand. The Academy was my effort to pass on some of the good fortune I'd enjoyed. By bringing together the best mathematicians and philosophers, I wanted to continue the noble enterprise that Socrates had begun. Also, there was always at the back

The star pupil of the Academy is depicted in the
Portrait of Aristotle by Joos van Gent, circa 1475.

of my mind the thought that philosophers, if they could be trained and somehow brought to political power, might end the troubles that beset the cities of my time. It would be wrong to think of the Academy as what you might call a school of political science, but I still harbored the thought that philosophical expertise might be engaged in the improvement of government.

Q. What was the curriculum at the Academy?

Let me outline what seemed to me to be the right course of study for a philosopher who might be destined to go on to a role in politics. For a period of ten years, from the age of twenty to thirty, students would concentrate on mathematics. First would come arithmetic, followed by plane geometry, and then solid geometry. The mathematical curriculum would climax with the study of mathematical idealizations of physics: the harmonics of strings, and the movements of heavenly bodies, or astronomy. After ten years of mathematical studies there would be five years of practice in dialectic, the question-and-answer technique of Socrates.

Keep in mind, though, that our studies were by no means restricted to a fixed curriculum. I suspect that you're familiar with the work of Aristotle, who, during twenty years at the Academy, delved deeply into a wide array of subjects, some of which were far removed from the core of mathematics and philosophy.

Q. I'm surprised by your emphasis on mathematics. Since your main goal was the advancement of philosophy, why would you lean so heavily on the study of numbers, shapes, and figures? These two

The School of Athens, a fresco by Raphael (1483–1520). This detail shows Euclid or Archimedes with students.

Plato wanted to carry on the teachings of Socrates (left) so that others might also experience the noble enterprise the great philosopher had begun.

studies seem far removed from one another.

The short answer is that mathematics more obviously relies on reason alone for its advancement. Although both philosophy and mathematics have the same reliance on reason, it's easier to see the connection when you're thinking abstractly about quantity and shape than it is when you're investigating justice and beauty and the good. When the right habits of mind are established by the study of mathematics, one can then more easily focus on the abstract natures that are the subject of philosophical reasoning.

Q. Remind me, please, how this course of study qualifies a person to rule a state.

You'll recall that dialectic, as practiced by Socrates, inquired into the nature of such things as wisdom, courage, temperance, justice, and the good itself. These are just the things that a ruler must understand clearly if he, or she, is to rule well. Even if the ruler is charged only to write the framework laws for a representative democracy, there's no hope of its being done well in the absence of a clear grasp of the good of the citizens and the state. Whether one is to rule directly, as a king, or to act as legislator, one must have the understanding that can be gained only through dialectic.

Q. We know that your own efforts in Sicily to apply your knowledge in practice came to nothing. Had you or your colleagues any better luck elsewhere?

It's hard in the short term to gauge success in establishing a polity. But several of my younger colleagues, including Eudoxus and Aristotle, did accept invitations to write laws for new cities, and I think their experiences may be counted as successful.

Q. Was this, then, your most satisfying achievement?

No. I have to say that what I found most gratifying was the electric atmosphere created by a community of scholars. We had there people who I think were the most brilliant mathematicians and philosophers in the Greek world. Advances were being made rapidly, especially in mathematics. The excitement was palpable. For a philosopher this was heaven on earth. Duty drew our gaze outside the Academy, but love drew it inward.

12

PLATONISM— THE THEORY OF FORMS

As an account of the nature of mathematics and philosophy Plato posited a realm of abstract natures or forms. Exactly what he meant by this has been much disputed by scholars. Throughout history there have been philosophers who have regarded themselves as Platonists, but among them there has been little agreement as to just what the core of the doctrine was. Similarly, those who have chosen to oppose Platonism have not always directed their criticisms at the same thing.

Q. The term "Platonism" is frequently used, in academic discussions at least. I understand that it refers to some very grand theory. What's the purpose of this theory? What is it meant to explain? And what does it assert?

There are actually two main purposes. The first is to explain how it is that Socratic dialectic can succeed as it does. The second is to counter the widespread subjective relativism of the sophists, such as Protagoras. Each of these seems to me equally important. You'll never understand my purely philosophical writings unless you keep both of these purposes constantly before your mind.

The dialectic of Socrates helps others gain knowledge by showing them where their theories fail.

I've already mentioned that a good many people regarded Socrates' dialectic as nothing more than a means of reducing its victims to a state of perplexity. Now, I have no doubt that Socrates' questioning can have this effect, but I'm confident that it can produce genuine knowledge. Examples can show that it does yield knowledge, but it's important to have an explanation as to why it does so. This is what Platonism was to explain.

Q. Remind me again how examples show that Socrates produces knowledge rather than just perplexity.

I mentioned before a simple example from the *Republic*, in which the nature of justice is discussed. We can see better the potential of Socrates' procedure by noting how he follows up his refutation of Cephalus's suggestion that justice is nothing but telling the truth and repaying what has been received. Cephalus himself doesn't want to continue, but his son Polemarchus is eager to inherit the argument. He sees what's gone wrong with his father's account and offers a revision of it that avoids its error.

Socrates is able to show that this account also fails, but for a different reason. A new, revised version of the son's definition is offered—but this is found to be mistaken in a new way. By stages like this the speakers are able to approach nearer and nearer to the truth. This improvement in their understandings is based entirely upon knowledge that they themselves already possessed.

Q. Well, if examples alone are enough to show that Socratic dialectic can be successful, why do you need a theory?

If there's no explanation for why something works, there's a natural tendency to suspect that the success is illusory. Magic appears to work, but we all know that the magician is really an illusionist. To persuade doubters, we need to show that Socrates is no illusionist. And anyway, it's intellectually unsatisfactory to know only that something works without knowing why it does.

Now for Protagoras and the relativists. Protagoras' complete statement is, "Man is the measure of all things, both the being of things that are and the not being of things that aren't." This implies that nothing is anything just by itself, but anything is what it is only to someone. To someone else it may appear otherwise, and, indeed, is otherwise to that person. There is, on this account, no distinction between *seeming* and *being*. If something seems to you right, then it is, to you, right. And if it seems to me wrong, then it is, to me, wrong. There's no such thing as simply being right or being wrong. And this applies to every property, not just right and wrong. If something seems to you a pig and seems to me a sheep, then to you it's a pig and to me it's a sheep. There's no such thing as being, just by itself, a thing of one kind or another.

So, if everything is as it appears, then false belief is impossible. If every belief must be true just because it's believed, then thought and reason are superfluous. Philosophy and every other intellectual discipline would have no purpose, as error would be impossible and truth would require no search. This extreme relativism is the antithesis of philosophy. Its widespread popularity is the bane of the true philosopher. As much as I cared about anything, I cared to extinguish the contagion of relativism.

Q. All right, I see why you wanted a theory, but just what is the theory?

You've probably heard it referred to as a theory of "forms," which is a little misleading because it seems to suggest that it's all about shapes. It would be better to think of it as a theory of natures or characters.

You remember the kind of question Socrates asked— what is it to be holy, for example, or to be righteous, or courageous, or beautiful? These you recognize to be inquiries into the natures of the holy, the righteous, the courageous, and the beautiful. Never mind the word, the theory is about these things and their discovery.

I guess I can best state the theory in a minute or two by reducing it to six fundamental propositions. First, for every kind there is a single nature common to things of the kind. Beautiful things all possess beauty, tall things all possess tallness, humans all possess humanity, and so on. Second, it's having these natures or characters that makes things be of the kinds that they are. Beauty makes beautiful things beautiful, tallness makes tall things tall, and so on. Third, these natures are necessarily as they are, and have necessary relations to one another. Beauty, for example, is always and necessarily the opposite of ugliness; wisdom is always and necessarily a virtue. Fourth, philosophy is, at least primarily, the inquiry into these natures, which isn't to say that every nature is a proper subject for philosophy. The nature of the pig, or of water, may well be beyond our knowledge—but those aren't the kinds of things we care about anyway. The fifth proposition is that it's by means of reason, and not our senses, that we discover the truth about these natures. And the last general principle is that this discovery is possible

"Beautiful things all possess beauty, tall things all possess tallness, humans all possess humanity, and so on." Here, the Panthenon is a timeless example of beauty, shown being restored in this 2008 photograph.

only because the inquirer had prior knowledge of these natures.

Q. A grand theory, to be sure, but I have a question about these things you prefer to call natures. Exactly where do they exist? If they are only in the things that have them, then they are not always or necessarily anything, since the things they are in are only transitory. And, if they're apart from the things that have them, then where on Earth, or in heaven, are they?

I notice that as you ask where they are, you gaze heavenward. If you keep that up, all you'll get is a crick in your neck. I think I've said that it's by thinking, and not by staring, that you'll find these things. Your incomprehension illustrates what I've been saying all along—that it's only after much study, and a long apprenticeship, that we're likely to be able to comprehend these natures adequately.

13

OUR WAY OUT OF THE CAVE

Among the many literary devices—myths, metaphors, and verbal images—that Plato used, the allegory of the cave is probably the most memorable and the most instructive. Introduced in the *Republic* as a simile for our need for education, it illustrates far more. In fact, in this one image Plato encapsulates almost his entire philosophy.

Q. Everyone who's in the least familiar with your work remembers the allegory of the cave. It remains vividly in mind, but I'm a little hazy as to its meaning. What exactly did you mean to convey?

Quite a few things, really—almost all of the important points that Socrates makes in the *Republic*. In the cave, if you recall, prisoners are chained up facing the back wall of the cave, and all they can see are shadows on the wall. The shadows are cast by puppets of humans and other animals held aloft by people walking back and forth on a parapet behind the prisoners. The cave is dimly lit by a fire behind these puppets. The prisoners represent the uneducated mass of humankind. The shadows are only dim representations of imitations of real things, but for the prisoners they are reality, and represent people's poor understanding of the nature of the things they see. The prisoner who's released and turned to

Plato's Cave, 16th century oil on panel. "Plato's Cave" is an allegory about knowledge and the quest for or the rejection of it.

face the fire, and the imitations whose shadows he'd taken to be real, represents everyone who has to face up to the errors in what he's learned.

The prisoner's forced, steep ascent out of the cave into the sunlight represents the difficulty of the education in mathematics that prepares one for philosophy. The reluctance of the prisoner to make the steep climb parallels the inclination of students to think that the hard work is not worth the effort. The bright sunlit world outside represents the abstract realm that reason, when properly exercised, can reveal to the soul. The prisoner, when acclimatized to the outside world, is like the philosopher who's mastered dialectic. And when the erstwhile prisoner has so adjusted his eyes that he can directly view the sun itself, he's like the philosopher who's grasped the nature of the good.

Q. That's quite a journey for this poor soul. I see how your story illustrates the need for, and the difficulty of, the education that you've prescribed. Are there any other lessons to be learned from this image?

To be sure. The quandary that the true philosopher faces can be seen here. Think for a minute about the difference between the life of the released prisoner and that of his former companions. His compassion for them in their miserable state—although they don't perceive themselves as miserable because they know nothing beyond their world of shadows—must move him to return to the cave and try to rescue them. When he tells them that their world is all illusion, and that the real world is something much greater and more interesting, they're bound to be skeptical. If they are fair-minded they may test his supposedly superior wisdom in the only way they know, by his quickness in recognizing shadows as they appear on the cave wall. Of course, his eyes will no longer be adjusted to the gloom of the cave, and his heart won't be in the game of identifying shadows. His poor performance will persuade the others that his claimed knowledge of a greater reality is bogus and they'll resent his superior pose. If they could get their hands on him, they'd kill him.

Q. Let me guess. You have Socrates' fate in mind here?

Of course. There were other motives operating in his execution, but the resentment of his exposure of false wisdom has to have been a major factor.

Q. A lot of this makes sense, but why doesn't the released prisoner, when he returns to the cave, just undo the shackles and let the others see for themselves?

This is an allegory—it's not meant to be taken literally. By talking with these people and trying to get them to understand, he is trying to undo the shackles. If you don't see these allegories, myths, and metaphors this way, then you'd better not read the dialogues. If you take everything I've written literally, then you'll misunderstand completely. You'll take me for a simpleton.

Q. I'm very sorry. Please excuse my lack of intellectual subtlety.

Of course. But try to do better.

14

MATHEMATICS AND THE SEARCH FOR TRUTH

A prominent contemporary French mathematician, Jean Dieudonné, has declared that almost all working mathematicians are Platonists. Despite this, and despite the widespread impression that mathematics is the natural home of Platonism, many modern mathematicians have rejected Platonist thinking. Geometry, at least, they suppose to contain no truth at all, let alone timeless and necessary truth. Plato has to explain the prominence of mathematics in his own philosophy and in the training that he prescribes as preparation for philosophy.

Q. You've emphasized the importance of mathematics in the education of philosophers. Why is it so important?

I have indeed praised mathematics for its use in preparing young people for the study of dialectic. But I don't want to give the impression that it's important only for that purpose. In itself mathematics is a fascinating and important subject. It is, if pursued properly, a paradigm of secure scientific knowledge. Anyone who's attained a grasp of it has in his or her mind a fine example of the kind of knowledge that every thinking person must cherish.

Socrates used reason to teach a truth about geometry.

Q. Are you thinking of its use in practical affairs, such as land measurement, bridge building, and carpentry?

No. Those uses of mathematics are important but too obvious to need mention. What I have in mind is mathematics as abstract and universal knowledge. A feature of real knowledge is that it must be true. Mathematics has this distinctive feature, that it's necessarily true. It's not just true in the way that the belief that sea water is undrinkable is true. What's true in mathematics couldn't be otherwise.

Consider, for example, a perfectly simple fact of arithmetic, that two plus three equals five. If you think for just a second about this you'll realize that it could not be otherwise. Nothing that anyone, even a god, could do would make two and three to be more or less than five.

Q. I've always been puzzled about this, but I know that many say that this line of thought is clearly wrong. They say it's very easy to show that two quarts of sand and three quarts of water do not, when mixed, amount to five quarts of wet sand. How do you reply?

This is important. We're dealing here with a complete misunderstanding of the nature of mathematics. You're talking about the result of pouring together two different substances. The results of the act of mixing are not the subject of mathematics. Mathematics says no more about what the resulting amount would be than it says about whether the result would be an explosion! The arithmetical proposition we're considering asserts only this about our quarts of sand and water: that so long as there are two quarts here and three more quarts there, there are five quarts altogether.

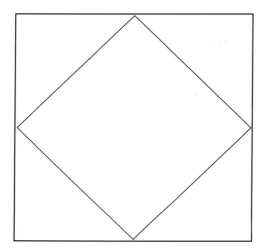

Plato's two squares guide a boy as he reasons through a problem: A square drawn on the diagonal of another must contain twice the area of the original.

It's perhaps not quite as easy to see that the same necessity obtains in geometry as in arithmetic. But consider the simple proposition that Socrates demonstrated to Meno in my dialogue of that name. He led Meno's uneducated slave boy to see that a square on the diagonal of a given square has twice the area of the given square. Try it for yourself—draw a square. Now draw another square on the diagonal of the first square. When the two squares are seen in this way it's easy to see that the second contains exactly four halves of the original. My point is not that this is true, but that nothing could possibly change the relationship between the two squares. As long as they are these squares and not some others, the ratio of the one to the other is unalterable.

Q. Now I'm a little confused. You've just invited me to draw a couple of diagrams and look at them. Doesn't that undermine your belief that it's by thought alone— by reason itself—that you recognize geometrical truths?

Sir Isaac Newton is one of the mathematical geniuses of the last millennium.

No. You've noticed a feature of geometrical thinking. A geometer does use diagrams as an aid, but every geometer knows that a drawn figure has imperfections. No drawn lines will be perfectly straight or uniformly curved. Nor will drawn lines ever be entirely without thickness. The theorems of geometry are about shapes whose boundaries are perfect. So, though diagrams are used in geometry, they are used only to bring to mind the shape in question. They are not themselves those very shapes.

Q. But if these abstract truths of your mathematics are independent of empirical facts, haven't you given away its utility in practical affairs?

Not at all. We can, if you wish, distinguish between pure and applied mathematics. We've been talking about pure mathematics. It can, of course, be applied to good purpose in very many cases. Consider an application that was well known even in my time—astronomy. Although the mathematics of the heavens was not known then, it was recognized that the movements there would be mathematically describable. Of course, the movements of the heavenly bodies couldn't be expected to conform exactly to the mathematical models. Nevertheless, the mathematics could very usefully be applied to bring about an understanding of the heavens. Mathematics is applicable to physical reality. It's just that one must be careful in the application.

Q. This does sound right. In fact, the mathematization of physical science over the past few centuries is generally thought to be the greatest advance in the history of science. One Isaac Newton is often regarded as the greatest genius of the last millennium for his success. But since you've said so much in praise of mathematics and of mathematicians, why did you in the *Republic* rate mathematical thinking as inferior to philosophy?

You recall that I've called philosophical reasoning dialectic. It's characteristic of dialectic that it treats every opinion as a hypothesis—something that must be subjected to sustained scrutiny before it's accepted. Mathematicians have all too often accepted their starting points—their axioms and definitions—as mere assumptions. They haven't subjected them to scrutiny, but have just assumed them to be adequate. From such assumptions they've been scrupulous in deducing consequences. But these consequences can have no more certainty than belongs to the assumed beginnings. Dialectic doesn't rely on assumptions. That's why I've regarded the one way of thinking as inferior to the other.

Q. I think I understand in a general way what you mean about mathematicians' reasoning. But what do you find inadequate in the foundations from which they proceed?

The most fundamental things with which they begin— numbers in arithmetic, and points, lines, and surfaces in geometry—are by no means adequately defined. If you were to study the history of mathematics you'd see that we have enormous difficulty in saying what a point is, what it is for a line to be straight, or what it is for lines to be parallel. And in arithmetic the unit, of which all other numbers are multiples, is quite perplexing. Although it's in essence single, we're inclined to say that it's twice one half, and so is dual. Such perplexities have not been resolved by the mathematicians.

Q. Perhaps these philosophical-sounding questions are treated lightly by mathematicians. But if their axioms and definitions don't contain actual errors, what's the harm in leaving them as they are? How will we be led astray if we follow out their consequences?

I've already mentioned one loss you suffer if you go this way.

You give up the opportunity to gain certain knowledge. If your definitions and axioms are not known to be certainly true, then what's deduced from them cannot be known with certainty. To give up so much without a struggle seems to me to be defeatist.

Beyond this, there may be an even greater price to pay for the careless treatment of the foundations on which mathematics is built. I greatly fear that this carelessness about the truth of the premises may lead some to think that it doesn't matter whether they are true. They may come to be regarded as no more than arbitrary starting points. In fact, I can imagine someone going so far as to suggest that they are treated as merely meaningless symbols that assert nothing either true or false. This would, in the case of geometry, open the way for a variety of "geometries." Each of these would begin from different "axioms" and "definitions," and none would be more true than any other. In this case not only certainty but truth as well would be given up.

Q. I don't know whether you're prescient or whether you've been peeking at a history of the mathematics of the past two centuries, but you've just described what has actually happened. Among those who took this deflated view of geometry was Albert Einstein, who is widely regarded as the greatest genius of the 20th century. How do you feel about the accuracy of your foreboding?

Forlorn! Well, not quite. I'm optimistic enough to think that most mathematicians will, like the French gentleman you mentioned earlier, be enchanted by the beauty of mathematics and by the thrill of discovery, and will be unwilling to forswear the search for truth.

15

PLATONISM RECONSIDERED?

n *Parmenides*, Plato gave to many readers the impression that, in his later years, he had second thoughts about his one grand theory—the theory of "forms," which we call Platonism. In this dialogue he had the venerable philosopher Parmenides raise several objections against young Socrates' Platonic theory. One of the arguments that Parmenides offers against Socrates is very similar to an argument that Plato's brilliant student Aristotle apparently regarded as fatal to Platonism. A great many scholars now agree with Aristotle and suppose that Plato too must have come to see his theory as refuted.

Q. Many modern readers have inferred from one of your later works that you had second thoughts about Platonism. They suggest that, because of objections you yourself raised, you abandoned your own theory. Did you really give it up?

I think this idea must come from a careless reading of the dialogue *Parmenides*. In that dialogue, Parmenides, as an old man, visits Athens from his home in Italy. He meets the youthful Socrates, who has already come to believe what you recognize as Platonism—that is, that all things

Bust of Parmenides of Elia. Parmenides of Elia questioned Socrates, recorded in Plato's *Parmenides*.

of a particular kind share in a single nature, or form, that's distinct from, and independent of, the things themselves.

Parmenides is impressed with the young man's cleverness, but raises several questions and reservations. When faced with these questions, the young Socrates is nonplussed. He's unable to answer the objections. Parmenides offers several arguments, but he warns the young man that he'll face many more.

I'm only guessing here, but I imagine that those who think I doubted my theory will have focused on just one of the objections that Parmenides raised. I suspect this because my own student, Aristotle, had misgivings about one aspect of the theory. Taking men as his example, Aristotle thought that if, in order to define what makes a man a man, you posit a single nature, "man," as separate from all actual men, then you'll need another nature (a "third man") to define what the first nature and all actual men have in common. But this would mean that what was supposed to be a single nature would be multiplied into two or more—and this is clearly at odds with my theory. One of the objections raised by Parmenides is similar to this. You can appreciate that this might be seen as troublesome to a Platonist.

Q. Then are the modern readers right? Should we see this dialogue as a repudiation of Platonism by Plato?

Not if you pay attention to the dialogue itself. The questions and objections on which your modern readers are fixated occur within an introductory portion. The main portion of the dialogue —three-quarters of it, in fact—is a demonstration by Parmenides of the sort of dialectic that young Socrates will need to learn in order to overcome objections to this theory. Naturally, any introduction to this demonstration must present some difficulties, and leave them unresolved.

George Grey Barnard's nineteenth century masterpiece *Struggle of the Two Natures in Man*; Aristotle had misgivings about Plato's theory on a single nature in man.

Quite apart from the context, you should note Parmenides' own assessment. After raising his objections and noting Socrates' uncertainty, he declares that Socrates' theory must be right. His mistake is only that he has begun philosophy too young, before he's been properly trained.

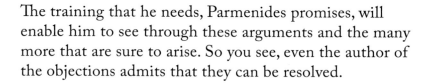

The training that he needs, Parmenides promises, will enable him to see through these arguments and the many more that are sure to arise. So you see, even the author of the objections admits that they can be resolved.

Q. But the dialogue leaves the objections unanswered. Won't you give me at least a clue as to what's wrong with them?

All right. Since you aren't a philosopher, and have obviously reached an age at which you're unlikely to become one, I'll answer that. I take it that even among the readers of your day it's well understood that Platonism is essentially a distinction between abstract natures—including numbers and shapes—and the things that possess these natures. The objections that Parmenides raises all seem to have this fault: they treat the abstract natures as if they were more like the things than they really are. The distinction between what's known only by reason and what's known only by the senses is fundamental. Parmenides' objections all seem to ignore this radical distinction.

Q. So far you've had only limited success in persuading later philosophers to recognize this distinction, and in promoting your political philosophy. Given what must seem to you the incomprehension of so many of your readers—all through the centuries, I mean—how do you feel about your life's work? Have you any large regrets?

I suppose you mean regrets about my own actions and the conduct of my life. None that weighs on me. Always in the back of my mind was the feeling that I must live up to the example set by Socrates. I should like to have taken an active part in politics, but it always seemed as if, as things were, one could not do that either honorably or safely. So, I retreated to the life of the mind, hoping that by introducing others to philosophy I would help create the situation in which honorable people could hope to bring about revolutionary political change. It was my good fortune that this duty that fell upon me corresponded perfectly to my own deepest personal desires. Philosophy had a hold on me from the moment I got to know Socrates, and it yielded the greatest pleasure and satisfaction.

Q. Did your withdrawal from active public life never make you feel as if you hadn't measured up to the example of Socrates in point of personal courage?

It's never right to ask a man whether he lacks courage. It didn't occur to me, though, that I fell short in this respect. Like others I did my military duty, and in the Assembly I defended an accused man whom no one else would defend, even at the risk of my own life. This isn't something that I dwell on, but I don't have the feeling that I should have risked more than I did.

Perhaps I could have done more during my life. But maybe it's enough for one man, in one lifetime, to have pointed the way that others may follow.

Q. Perhaps it is. Thank you, Plato, and farewell.

GLOSSARY

Academy: A gathering of intellectuals, guided by Plato, for the study of philosophy, mathematics, and astronomy. It was founded sometime after 390 BCE and stayed in existence into the sixth century CE.

allegory: A story, poem, or picture that can be interpreted to reveal a hidden meaning.

Acropolis: An ancient citadel on a rocky hill in Athens, which contains the remains of several architecturally or historically significant buildings.

apology: A justification or a defense of a position. Plato's *Apology* is a recounting of a defense put forth by Socrates before the court in Athens.

Arab: A member of the Semitic people of the Arabian Peninsula.

aristocracy: The highest class in any society, especially those holding hereditary titles.

calumny: Making false statements to damage the reputation of another person.

demagogue: A political or religious leader who seeks support by appealing to popular desires and prejudices rather than by using rational arguments.

dialectic: A discussion and reasoning by dialogue to expose false beliefs and discover truth.

dialogue: A conversation or a discussion to resolve a problem.

forms: A theory that postulates the existence of a level of reality or "world" inhabited by the ideal or archetypal forms of all things and concepts.

hermaphrodite: A human that has both male and female body parts.

Hindu: A follower of Hinduism, the primary religion of India. It includes the worship of many gods and the belief in reincarnation.

intransigent: Unwilling to compromise or to abandon a position or attitude.

junta: A military group that forms a government after taking over by force.

Neoplatonists: Those such as Christians who believe in a single source from which all existence emanates and with which an individual soul can be mystically united.

oligarchy: A form of government in which power is vested in a small group or a dominant class.

pandemic: Occurring over a wide geographic area and affecting a large percentage of the population.

Parthenon: A temple on the Acropolis dedicated to Athena.

philosophy: The study of ideas about knowledge, truth, and the nature and meaning of life.

Platonic: A striving toward a love of spiritual or ideal beauty. Can mean today a relationship free from sensual desire.

Platonism: A philosophy stressing that actual things are copies of transcendent ideas and that these ideas are the objects of true knowledge apprehended by reminiscence.

polity: A form or process of civil government or constitution.

rhetoric: The art of expressive or persuasive speaking or writing.

rump: A small or inferior remnant or offshoot.

scion: A person born into a rich, famous, or important family.

skepticism: A philosophical approach that questions the possibility of certainty and leads to ambiguity or doubt. This leads to relativism, which says that points of view have no absolute truth.

Sophists: Traveling philosopher teachers who taught rhetoric and public speaking. They were criticized for being more concerned with popularity for the sake of economic gain than with the truth.

Spartan: An inhabitant of the city state of Sparta, whose inhabitants known for their courage, self-discipline, and austere lifestyle.

treatise: A written work that deals thoughtfully and comprehensively with a subject.

Trinitarian: The belief that Plato began to doubt and abandon Platonism and the teachings of Socrates.

Unitarian: The belief that there is a single philosophy consistently held by Plato in all his works.

For FURTHER INFORMATION

Books

Gow, Mary. *The Great Philosopher Plato and His Pursuit of Knowledge*. Berkeley Heights, NJ: Enslow Publishing, 2010.

Gill, Christopher, ed. *The Symposium by Plato*. New York, NY: Penguin Classic, 2003.

Kraut, Richard, ed. *The Cambridge Companion to Plato*. Cambridge, England: Cambridge University Press, 1992.

Melling, David. *Understanding Plato*. Oxford, England: Oxford University Press, 1988.

Rouse, W. H. D., and Matthew S. Santirocco, eds. *Great Dialogues of Plato*. New York, NY: Signet Classic, 2008.

Website

Standard Encyclopedia of Philosophy

plato.stanford.edu/search/searcher.py?query=Plato

Stanford University provides references for statements made or beliefs held by Plato.

INDEX

ABOUT *the* AUTHOR

DONALD R. MOOR is a professor emeritus in philosophy at Portland State University in Portland, Oregon. He earned his bachelor of arts degree from the University of British Columbia and his Ph.D. from the University of Oregon. His interests include the nature of philosophy and logic, geometry, and arithmetic, all elements of Platonism.

ROBERT M. PIRSIG (foreword) is an American writer and philosopher. Among his most famous works are *Zen and the Art of Motorcycle Maintenance* and *Lila: An Inquiry into Morals*.